Keys to Third Heaven

Using Third Heaven Revelation

to Impact a World

By

Sharnael Wolverton

Endorsements

"This is the year of Sharnael's rising! This is her running year!"

Graham Cooke
Future Training Institute

"The church is in a fresh new day. Divine opportunities are at the door in an unprecedented way. Likewise, there are also many new and fresh faces emerging with holy desperation in their soul and passion for God's kingdom. Sharnael Wolverton of Swiftfire Ministries International is one such example!"

Paul Keith Davis
WhiteDove Ministries

"Sharnael has been called to preach, teach and prophesy, there is an apostolic seed of anointing inside of her and she has a prophet's mantle upon her. The working of her faith will cause a response from the Heavens!"

Patricia King
Extreme Prophetic

"Some are gifted with a *prophetic message* for their hour; others have a *prophetic gift* and can speak a personal word over your life with great accuracy. Sharnael is that rare person with a *prophetic life*, which includes both a message to the hour and a gift for personal ministry. Combined with her prophetic acumen, Sharnael's single minded, whole hearted devotion to Jesus makes her a trusted voice in my life and one I encourage others to listen to as well."

Lance Wallnau
Lancelearning Group

"Sharnael offers something needed for the church: a fresh perspective with new inventive ideas that awaken people to how deep the kingdom of God can really be. She has a prophetic perspective about both the church world and the secular world. Her supernaturally natural Biblical presentation in her meetings coupled with her writing style set her apart in this day where people are longing for not just new voices but a radical cry of intimacy and reality of who God really is."

Shawn Bolz
Expression58 Ministries

"Sharnael Wolverton has a passion to see the kingdom of God extended through prophecy, signs and wonders. With her bold, simple faith in action, she is blazing a trail for many to follow."

Stacey Campbell
Revival Now! Ministries

In a time when a generation needs connection with God's Spirit, Sharnael is uniquely gifted to provide. Her sincere desire to train people and reach out is infused with God's love, grace, and compassion.

Doug Addison
InLight Connection

"I am struck by several things in Sharnael, but especially her hunger for God and her passion for the prophetic. Her desire to see the supernatural poured out in the earth is very refreshing. Sharnael is truly a "Daughter of Destiny" called to impact her generation for God."

Larry Randolph
Larry Randolph Ministries

"I deeply appreciate Sharnael's honesty, openness to the Holy Spirit and her burning devotion to her King. May she carry the fire of Christ throughout the nations to the glory of His name! I warmly commend Sharnael to you as a minister of the Gospel of our Lord Jesus."

Catherine Brown
Gatekeepers

"Sharnael Wolverton's book will encourage anyone who is seeking to walk deeper in the revelatory."

Bobby Conner
Eagles View Ministries

Keys to Third Heaven

Using Third Heaven Revelation

to Impact a World

By

Sharnael Wolverton

swiftfire publishing
1113 S. Range Ave. Suite 110, Box 333 Denham Springs, La 70726
225-791-7696 swiftfire.org

International Standard Book Number:
978-09796622-0-1
First Printing June 2007

Editor: Arlene Brown
Contributing Editors: Charlotte Bouzigard &
Will Steele
Cover Graphics: Sharnael and Stephen Wolverton
Key and Eagle Images: Robert Bartow Bartowimages.com
Interior Design: Don Pennington

Printed in the United States of America

To contact the author about speaking at your church or
conference or
For more information on swiftfire resources go to
www.swiftfire.org

Published By
swiftfire publishing
Denham Springs, La 70726

Dedications

To Him, first and foremost—the author and finisher of my dreams, my journey, and my physical and spiritual life; may I always be effective in You, not wasting a single drop of grace.

I am what I am by the grace of God, and His grace to me was not without effect (1 Corinthians 15:10).

To my husband, Stephen, my parents Chris and Connie Wolverton, and my sister Karmen, I cannot begin to thank you for your unending support and encouragement to me over the years. You have always allowed me to be and to become who I am and you have always encouraged me to believe that there are absolutely no limits to what God can do through me. You have been there for me in every way and you have sacrificed much for the call. Thank you for your gifts of unfailing and unconditional love, and thank you for always encouraging me to move higher in Him.

To my girls, Shaen, Søren, and baby Sharnael "Shön" you are so beautiful in Christ. May you always reach to the heavens to be everything you can be and do everything you can do during your time here on earth.

*I tell you the truth, anyone who has faith in me will do what I have been doing. He will **do even greater things than these**, because I am going to the Father* (John 14:12).

May we all do greater things than these.

Acknowledgements

I don't know where to begin. The road has been fun and sometimes a bit nuts. There are many people to thank along the way.

Of course, my Heavenly Father and family as I have mentioned previously. Without you I am nothing!

To Arlene Brown, Charlotte Bouzigard, and Will Steele for your editing and encouragement! Special thanks to Don and Mary Jo Pennington without your help it would have been much more difficult to see this "baby" birthed!

To Marguerite and Phillip Scardina, Nancy Flowers, Dana and Byron Cammack, Caroline Boudreau, Ann Devall, Nick and Jvona Jambon and Maylia and Jude Trahan: thank you for your unfailing love, friendship and support to me and this ministry. All of you have poured in to my life in many ways. I pray the Lord would give you and your families back a double portion.

Thanks so much to the entire Swiftfire Ministries International team.

Thank you for your ***loyalty*** to me and the vision of Swiftfire! Most of all thank you for your service to the King!

Special thanks to our Swiftfire Partners and Intercessors you keep the dream alive. Thanks for your obedience to Him.

Elaine Ulik, thanks for giving me my first word that started this ball rolling! May you be refreshed in your House of Prayer.

Bob Jones, thanks for introducing me to Swift, the Golden Eagle and for helping me receive confirmation of who I am in Christ. The biggest turning point in my life so far occurred when God led me to you and your ministry. Your ministry to God and others inspires me and your words are always perfectly on time. Thanks to you and to your beautiful new wife, Bonnie!

Joy Parrott, Doug Addison, Patricia King, Graham Cooke, Paul Keith and Wanda Davis, Bobby Conner, John Paul Jackson, Larry and Laura Randolph, Kari Browning, Wes and Stacey Campbell, and Shawn Bolz: at times over long distances, at times in person, and sometimes in dreams, some of you are very aware of this and some of you without knowing have helped change my life, given me keys and pointed me in the right direction through your own dedication to Christ. For this, I thank you.

To all of you mentioned above and to the many I could not list—you know who you are.

He who refreshes others will himself be refreshed Proverbs 11:25b).

May you all be refreshed in a mighty way for all you have given to me, to my family, and to this ministry.

Foreword

Sharnael Wolverton is a woman of great character and integrity, so why wouldn't the pages of this book be likewise? *"Keys to Third Heaven"* is compelling, convicting, challenging, and encouraging. Sharnael uses deep insights with a clear translation. The content of this book is filled with dreams, visions, examples, and stories that equip us to impact the earth one by one.

Whether you are new to the prophetic or are seasoned in this gift, you will benefit from this book. Sharnael imparts much needed wisdom, to transform the pathetic into the prophetic. It is like a swift arrow that pierces through the soul and spirit rightly dividing the Word of Truth, bringing life and transformation to you and those around you. I highly recommend Sharnael and this book to you!

Joy Parrott
Joy Parrott Ministries Author of *"Parables in the Night Seasons; Understanding Your Dreams"* and *"Watchman, Watchman, What of the Night?"*

Why I wrote this book

In February 2005, the Lord gave me a dream. In the dream He handed me a book. I knew when He handed it to me that it was more than a book. It was a commission. I woke up knowing that I had a responsibility to write but I wanted and needed a clear sense of timing.

I told my husband, Stephen, the dream and he laughed.

Why did he laugh? His response was tender but honest, "Honey, You have been saying that you were going to write this book since I met you ten years ago…I'll believe it when I see it."

He was so right.

After years of great intentions to pen (or type) the revelations that God has given to me, I realized that time was going by and these things were not being recorded. Goal - action = nothing but intention.

Three weeks later I went to a meeting in Mesa, Arizona, that was sponsored by Patricia King's Extreme

Prophetic Ministry. Within half an hour of walking in the door, Patricia[1] prophesied to me that she "saw a book."

She also saw me writing revelations God had given me for this book, the Internet and other publications.

Within a few days I had another dream. In this dream, I was in a glass elevator with a friend of mine, Meg Jones. There were also a couple of other people I did not recognize. The elevator shot up to the heavens very, very fast and very, very high.

The elevator went so fast and so high that I clutched the arms of the women standing next to me. I held my breath and shut my eyes. I could feel my stomach drop as we went higher, yet I could also see myself standing there with my eyes shut terrified as the other women kind of smiled, understanding "the process."

I peeked a few times and saw the clouds and the city below. Just as I began to get comfortable the glass elevator started slowly moving down.

As it came down, I could see the numbers of the floors getting lower and lower until it finally stopped on the fourth floor. (In dream interpretation the number four can represent creative works) I knew there was no getting off this floor for a while. I realized God had sent

---

[1] Patricia King
Extreme Prophetic
Po Box 1017
Maricopa, AZ 85239
www.extremeprophetic.com

me to heaven, imparted to me, and He was now requesting that I pen these things down for Him.

I knew I had a choice. It wasn't anything forced. I also knew that my heart had longed for this moment. It was now truly a reality. Something within me leapt with excitement. It was my heart burning forth in desire to please Him with a pen.

I pray Lord, that I would represent You well. I pray that You, the Creator of the universe, working through me, would help me create for You and Your people in order to bring change—lasting eternal change—for the sake of Your kingdom.

Table of Contents

Chapter		Page
	Introduction	23
1	Visions: "See and Say, Speak and Spell Or Dig and Decree	27
2	Visions of "Dust" Boy	35
3	Psychic or Prophetic Voice?	51
4	A More Excellent Way	59
5	How Can We Remove The Stumbling Blocks?	69
6	An Agent Of Change	81
7	False Prophets And Bad Fruit	87
8	The Wrong Stuff	93
9	Second Heaven Information vs Third Heaven	99
10	Only Second Heaven Information?	109
11	Any Two Year Old Can See And Say	117
12	All By Myself	123
13	Conclusions	129
14	Homework	131

Introduction

On our prophetic journey there are layers of revelation. Over the last year, the Lord has given me specific keys through several visions that have changed my perspective and transformed my mind regarding the prophetic ministry.

These perspectives can help you too, and accelerate you to higher levels than you have gone before. (Sounds a bit like a space movie, huh?) I firmly believe that if you take these keys and bury them in the good soil of your heart you will see a crop yielding a hundred, sixty or thirty times what was sown, just as Jesus says in Matthew 13:8–9:

"Still other seed fell on good soil, where it produced a crop—a hundred, sixty or thirty times what was sown. He who has ears, let him hear."

In verse 11–16 He continues:

He replied, The knowledge of the secrets of the kingdom of heaven has been given to you, but not to them. Whoever has will be given more, and he will have an abundance. Whoever does not have, even what he has will be taken from him. That is why I speak to them in parables:

Though seeing, they do not see; though hearing, they do not hear or understand.

In them is fulfilled the prophecy of Isaiah:

You will be ever hearing but never understanding; you will be ever seeing but never perceiving.

For this people's heart has become calloused; they hardly hear with their ears, and they have closed their eyes.

Otherwise they might see with their eyes, hear with their ears, understand with their hearts and turn, and I would heal them.

But blessed are your eyes because they see, and your ears because they hear.

For I tell you the truth, many prophets and righteous men longed to see what you see but did not see it, and to hear what you hear but did not hear it.

It is my belief that many of us are not seeing and hearing as well as we could be.

According to this passage it is because they—the prophets and righteous people—"do not have."

Why do they not have? Maybe because what they have been taught is false? Maybe because when they were taught there was a mixture of truth and soulish opinion? Or maybe because when they were introduced to the truth, either by man or by the Spirit, they did not regard these truths as valuable. They may have allowed the truths to fall on rocky places or among thorns to be scorched and choked.

We do not want to be one of the ones who "do not have." We want to have, have, have, so more can be given to us!

I firmly believe that if we will take the keys found in these next few pages and if we will apply them to our lives, then more will be given to us. What do I mean by more? I mean more revelation and more keys for our lives and for the lives of others.

I also believe that beyond the "more" that is given, we will also be given ears to hear more clearly than ever before and eyes to see more clearly than we can imagine.

I pray that the eyes of your heart will be open to hear what the Spirit longs to speak to you today.

And I pray that these truths will be planted in the best soil of your heart for a super-sized crop!

His,
Sharnael

CHAPTER 1

See and Say, Speak and Spell or Dig and Decree

In my travels around the world, I run into all kinds of people involved in the prophetic ministry. Some are brand new while others have been in this for years. Unfortunately, one thing I find common in many situations is that people are using their prophetic gift as a weapon against others.

Yes, the prophetic is a weapon, but it should be used as a tool or weapon against the enemy, not against those of us trying to remain on the same team, and especially not against the world!

See and Say Vision

In February 2004, I had a series of visions that

dramatically changed my perspective of the prophetic ministry as a whole.

In the first vision, the Lord stood before me holding a toy that I was very familiar with. It was a toy called *See and Say* that I played with as a child. Do you remember this toy? You would pull a string and an arrow turned around in circles until it landed on a picture and then it would say what the picture was.

He showed me a picture of a two-year-old child pulling the string of the toy. It landed on a horse. The child pointed to the horse and said "Horsy." Then He showed me the same two-year-old pulling the string a second time. I watched the arrow land on a dog this time. The child said "Doggy."

The Lord looked at me in a very serious way and said to me, *"Any two-year-old can See and Say."*

He then showed me another common game from my childhood called the *Speak and Spell*. To play *Speak and Spell* you would be asked to spell a word and the game would spell the word back to you. The game would talk to you and tell you if the word was spelled correctly or not. It would either say, "That is correct, now spell…" or, "That is *in*correct, try again. Spell…"

The Lord said, *"When you See and Say, it leaves room to Speak and Spell."*

One of the definitions of spell is to *curse someone*. The Lord was definitely trying to tell me something!

In other words, when we prophetic people point our fingers and state what seems obvious to us—for instance "sin", "lust", or "You are running from God," (just to name a few recent ones I have heard) we can actually be putting a spell or a curse on someone.

God was also trying to tell me that it was time to grow up and mature in the area of the prophetic. We as leaders can point and state the obvious easily but it takes spiritual maturity to hear the heart of God for someone.

Bewitch

Another definition of spell is to *bewitch someone*.

Galatians 3:1a says:

You foolish Galatians! Who has bewitched you?

Why did Paul ask this?

Because, after all of Paul's teaching and pouring out to them, someone had come in and turned the people back to their old ways of thinking and doing. To bewitch someone is basically to con them into something other than the truth.

In other words, "Foolish Galatians, who has come in and influenced you to come into agreement with something other than the Spirit of Truth?"

We have to be very careful when we minister to people. We want them to line up with God's heart and vision. We want them to remember *who* they really are.

We do not just tell them what they are doing wrong.

They already know that! They want to hear that they are okay. They want to know that God loves them just exactly where they are and that there is hope for them to reflect His perfect destiny in their lives.

Gentle Restoration

Our job is to restore people's hearts to the Father, and to restore them to their true destiny and calling.

*Brothers, if someone is caught in a sin, you who are spiritual should **restore** him **gently** (Galatians 6:1a).*

The word *restore* in this context according to Strong's Exhaustive Concordance 2596 means "to mend what has been broken; to strengthen; to make one what he ought to be; and to fit, equip."

The word *gently* according to Strong's 4235 means "gentleness, mildness, meekness."

We are to love people gently back into the arms of the Father.

Philippians 4:5a says:

Let your gentleness be evident to all.

Because of our giftings, we as prophetic people sometimes see things that may not be as noticeable to others. In fact, they may be extremely obvious to us, but that does not give us license to *spell* out the things that we see.

The Lord says, "*That is incorrect. Try again.*"

Treasure Finders

Instead of pointing out what we see, we need to search the matter out. We should request the Lord's hand in allowing us to see His vision for the person He has placed in our realm. We are responsible to represent the Lord as much as we possibly can. We are to reflect Him. This means that we need to dig deep and find the treasure in the person. We must dig until we find the destiny the Lord has for this person and speak it out!

We are not to speak what we see on the surface, instead we are to dig deep as treasure finders so we can speak forth what God says about His children and the world. After all, *"God so loved the **world"*** (John 3:16). He doesn't even mention the church!

See and Decree or See and Pray

Sometimes the Lord is showing us things in order for us to pray. Instead of *See and Say*, which leaves room for *Speaking and Spelling*, we may need to *See and Decree* or *See and Pray*!

Many times, the Lord will reveal secrets of heaven for us to pray. He is allowing us to become a part of someone's transformation through our silent prayers for the person. This takes incredible maturity but the Lord is asking us to grow up and become a part of the solution, not a part of the problem. He wants to trust that we can hold these things in our hearts and pull the people from darkness to light through prayer and declarations to the heavens.

Can He trust you? Are you really trust worthy? Let's see!

Think on this

1. What part in this chapter stands out to you the most?

2. Do you consider yourself a gentle person? If not, ask the Lord to show you specific ways in which you can demonstrate gentleness in someone's life this week. Record some of them below.

Prayerful Consideration

Lord, help us in this matter. Give us eyes to see and ears to hear as we continue reading these passages. We want to move forward in you. Give us keys to do so.

Amen

CHAPTER 2

Vision of "Dust" Boy

The Lord gave me a picture in February 2004 of a young boy, similar to the boy in a popular comic strip who walked around in his own cloud of dust. In the next scene, a "prophetic man" came over to him, pointed at him and said, "Dust." (See illustrations on pages 36-44)

As this word was spoken, the dust cloud around the boy grew much larger than it was at first. His face grew much heavier, and much darker. He began to slump over.

I saw in the spirit several small doors all around this boy. The doors were opened as he came into agreement with the "dust" word spoken over him. Through the doors came arrows that hit the center of his chest as he stood there like a target. These arrows were marked *confusion, loneliness, depression, hopelessness, shame, hate, suicide,* and others. The arrows represented demonic influences that had been released to torment and harass this young man—the very doors "Mr. Prophetic" guy helped open! This "prophetic word" brought confusion, shame, deep wounds, and depression. Because the cloud grew so big, it actually encased him. This caused his ability to hear and understand God weaken as the cloud almost completely separated him from the heavens like a thick ceiling.

In the last scene, a **true** prophetic person came to the same boy. This time the prophetic person dug deep. He looked deep within the boy's heart, past the cloud and past the obvious. He saw with spiritual eyes and heard with spiritual ears what the Father had to say about this little child of His.

Most importantly, the prophetic person asked the Lord, "What would You have me say?" And, "How would You have me say it?" "What would bring You Glory?" "What would bring this person into a better understanding of who You are to Him and who You are in Him?"

Of course, this prophetic person saw the surface "dust" but as he called forth those treasures and dreams within the boy's depths, they were birthed to the surface of his heart, cleaning out all the "yuck" in the process.

Then, a strange and beautiful thing happened—a flicker of light ignited within his heart! Hope was renewed. Life surfaced again and the cloud *dispelled*. He felt the love of the Lord in spite of his dusty state. Even more exciting was that the dust between him and the Father was also *di*spelled, leaving an open heaven for direct communication. Suddenly, he felt a lift. Suddenly, he could receive love, words of life, encouragement, strength, and freedom.

To Sum Up This Vision

In the first scene, the boy already had some dust in his life, but once it was confirmed it **magnified**. The picture the Lord gave me showed the boy as a victim with a large target on his chest after the "word" came forth. The doors all around him now became wide open. Coming from these doors were arrows of demonic influence and harassment. This "prophetic voice" had helped opened doors for demonic harassment and influence to a greater degree than before. With these spirits of shame, confusion, disgrace, death, loneliness, depression, etc. coming down for the attack, the boy was actually in a worse state than **before** the guy ministered to him.

The cloud grew into such darkness all around him that his ability to connect with heaven was even weaker. His ability to sense, hear, feel or see the Lord's guidance for his life was absolutely worse then five minutes prior. The cloud caused a terrible separation from the love of God he so desperately needed to know was available to him.

In the second scene, the prophetic person called forth things that were not (to the human eye) as though they were. (Paul speaks about this in Romans 4:17.) These treasures were no surprise to the prophetic man or to God. And to the boy? They were his inward dreams unspoken to anyone. They were his childhood visions, his fondest memories, his deep imaginations, and the hope of his calling. The truth and love of God dispelled all the darkness and made a highway open for this boy to communicate with heaven in a tangible way once again. The desires of his heart could now come out from where they were and move forward!

Like the prodigal son in the pigsty, he suddenly saw himself for who he was and even did something about it! "I am the son of a king! What am I doing here?"

Illustration #1

If you are interested in ordering the power point version of these illustrations go to swiftfire.org for more information.

Illustration #2

Illustration #3

Illustration #4

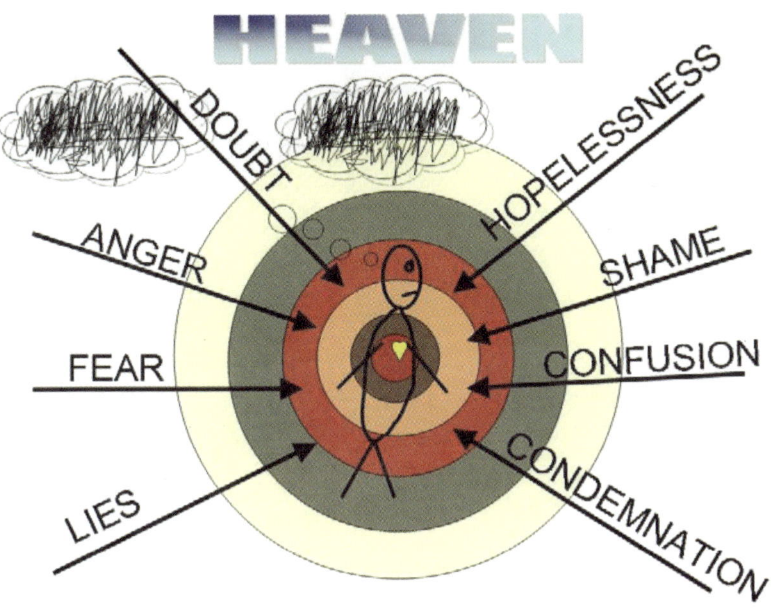

Illustration #5

Illustration #6

Illustration #7

Illustration #8

Illustration #9

Think on this

1. Which part of this chapter stands out to you the most?

2. Have you ever seen the prophetic gift demonstrated as it was in the first example, where the prophetic man spoke the word "dust" over the boy?

3. If you have, what was the result of the ministry time that you remember?

4. Has anyone ever used this particular method when ministering to you? How did it make you feel?

Prayerful Consideration

Lord, help us to forgive those who have used their prophetic gifts incorrectly in our lives. We submit those situations and people to You for Your care and healing. We long to move forward in our own lives and destiny. Help us speak Your words of truth to everyone we come in contact with.

Amen

CHAPTER 3

Psychic or Prophetic Voice?

I once heard John Paul Jackson[2] of Streams Ministries say, "A prophetic voice calls forth things that are not as though they are, but a psychic calls forth things that are as though they are not. "

Let me rephrase this:

A prophetic voice calls forth things that are not (yet to the human eye) as though they are, but a psychic calls forth things that are (the deep treasures within) as though they are not (the truth of God for one's life or who they really are).

Last time I looked, God has not called us to be psychics. Satan uses psychics to bewitch people.

---

[2] John Paul Jackson
Streams Ministries International
P.O. Box 550
North Sutton, NH 03260
www.streamsministries.com

Now don't get me wrong, I love and feel called to the hearts of the people in the New Age movement. Some psychics can actually have a true **gift** from God. The bottom line is what is their ***source***?

I believe that many are unaware that people can use a gift from God to channel a demonic source. Something more tangible, for example, would be a musician who is gifted by God but inspired by and guided by a demonic source. Psychics or New Age followers, for the most part, like us, may be thinking in their mind that they are helping people when they are actually ignorant to the powerful destruction they can bring.

Hosea 4:6 says:

"My people are destroyed from lack of knowledge."

The gift is from God it is the source we need to be sure of. Knowledge *really is* power. We need to be open to learning what it is God wants for us in order to be effective for the Kingdom.

In the Old Testament, the prophets spoke more freely in the "hard word" area. You see it all over the place. I believe this was because at that time the Holy Spirit had not yet been poured out to convict people of sin.

With the combination of the resurrection of Christ and the power given at Pentecost, we have two new things that Old Testament believers did not have:

1.Grace

2.The Holy Spirit

We all have the opportunity to hear and be convicted by the Holy Spirit because of Christ's resurrection. (John 15:26)

People already know they have sin in their lives, especially prodigals! What they want to know is how to get free from it and that God loves them just where they are. What they want to know is that there is still an opportunity for change and that there is power to do so.

First Corinthians 14: 1–3 says:

*Follow the way of love and eagerly desire spiritual gifts, **especially the gift of prophecy**. For anyone who speaks in a tongue does not speak to men but to God. Indeed, no one understands him; he utters mysteries with his spirit. But everyone who prophesies speaks to men for their **strengthening, encouragement and comfort**.*

My conviction is that New Testament prophets (or anyone moving in the gift of prophecy) are to be people of grace and love. Rarely do you see a prophetic word given in rebuke or correction in the New Testament, and especially to a pre-Christian. I am not dismissing counsel (that is different) or the relational guidelines found in Matthew 18:15–35, but Jesus' rebuke was usually reserved for the Pharisees and Sadducees. These were the only guys Jesus was ever mad at. Why? Because they themselves were bewitched and bewitching!

I am not saying that prophetic voices should not be truthful, nor am I saying that prophetic voices should not follow the Matthew 18 guidelines. Let's read them:

Mathew 18:15–17

If your brother sins against you, go and show him his fault, just between the two of you. If he listens to you, you have won your brother over.

But if he will not listen, take one or two others along, so that 'every matter may be established by the testimony of two or three witnesses.'

If he refuses to listen to them, tell it to the church; and if he refuses to listen to even to the church, treat him as you would a pagan or a tax collector.

Let's look again at the first part. "If your *brother* sins against you..." The word brother here indicates **relationship.** There needs to be proper relationship established before we go around correcting people.

When relationship and love are established, there is an understanding that what you have to say may be hard to hear, but you say it because you honestly have the best interest of the person at heart. You truly care and they know it. They feel it. They trust you and value your concern for them.

They may not respond perfectly all the time to what you bring to their attention, but when your words are attached with love and relationship it may cause them to think about it.

The word brother also indicates that this person may be in fact a brother in Christ, meaning He is open to spiritual things. He has had his eyes opened to truth. Trying to correct people that you do not have relationship with is difficult, and trying to correct people that don't have ears to hear **truth** is even more of a challenge.

Think on this

1. Which part of this chapter stands out to you the most?

2. Have you ever felt "bewitched" after an encounter with someone?

3. What was your response?

Prayerful Consideration

Lord help us to have Your knowledge and truth. I pray You will guide us every step of the journey towards You and Your plan for us. We desire to fully know You. Lord help us to use the gift of prophecy with care and love.

Amen

CHAPTER 4

A More Excellent Way

It is not by coincidence that 1 Corinthians 14:1 comes directly after 1 Corinthians 13, the popular "love chapter."

First Corinthians 12 speaks of the gifts too, as well as the five-fold ministry.

The last verse of 1 Corinthians 12:31 states:

But eagerly desire the greater gifts. And now I will show you the most excellent way.

The scriptures following go directly into the "love chapter."

In other words, yes, gifts are super and needed. But God is saying *Now let me show you the most excellent way*, namely the use of position/function (five-fold ministry) and the spiritual gifts filtered through and amplified with l-o-v-e.

What a combination!

When we mess with God's children we are going to be accountable for how we treat them and where we lead them.

In Luke 17:1–3a (NKJV) Jesus says to His disciples:

"It is impossible that no offenses should come, but woe to him through whom they do come! It would be better for him if a millstone were hung around his neck, and he were thrown into the sea, than that he should offend one of these little ones. Take heed to yourselves.

The word *offend* here is Strong's 4625, meaning "to put a stumbling block or impediment in the way upon which another may trip and fall, to cause a person to begin to distrust one whom he ought to trust and obey."

I heard a teaching by a dear man of God that I highly respect named Paul Keith Davis[3] where he describes "Angels that Gather." These angels are sent forth to remove the stumbling blocks and hindrances from our paths. Once this is done, we can then move more freely on a clear path toward to our destiny.

What if these stumbling blocks had to be removed because of all the Christians who put them there?

What if because of all our careless words and attitudes

---

[3] Paul Keith Davis
WhiteDove Ministries
P.O. Box 2153
Foley, AL 36535
www.whitedoveministries.com

God has to actually send angelic help to undo the mess we have made?

We do not want to be the ones causing roadblocks between people, our Father, and their destiny in Him.

In the New International Version of the bible the word used for offend is **confusion**.

If we provoke fear, shame and unrest into "these little ones" we are helping open doors for confusion to enter into their lives.

Galatians 5:10b says:

The one who is throwing you into confusion will pay the penalty, whoever he may be.

It sounds like God means business, doesn't it?

The word *confusion* in this verse according to Strong's 5015, means "to strike one's spirit with fear or dread, to cause an inward commotion, to perplex in the mind of one by suggesting doubts to stir up trouble and unrest."

If we bewitch others, whether Christian or pre-Christian, into coming into agreement with the enemy and the "dust" state they are in, we rob them of the truth and the destiny of who they are in Christ.

What we want to do is show others who they *really* are and guide them into His agreement in order for alignment to take place and spiritual fruit to come to its fullness in their lives.

The goal is **always** transformation.

Matthew 12:36 says:

But I say unto you, that every idle word that men shall speak, they shall give account thereof in the day of judgment (KJV).

The word *idle* in this verse, according to Strong's 2041, means "barren, shunning the labor of which one ought to perform, lazy, leisurely."

We must be so careful not to speak careless **barren** words. Words with no life are death and words with no fruit are barren.

The words of the wicked lie in wait for blood, but the speech of the upright rescues them (Proverbs 12:6).

Reckless words pierce like a sword, but the tongue of the wise brings healing (Proverbs 12:18).

A word aptly spoken is like apples of gold in settings of silver (Proverbs 25:11).

Your words have supported those who stumbled; you have strengthened faltering knees (Job 4:4).

*Do not let any unwholesome talk come out of your mouths, but only what is **helpful** for building others up according to **their needs** that it may benefit those who listen* (Ephesians 4:29).

*The Sovereign Lord has given me **an instructed tongue**, to **know the word that sustains the weary*** (Isaiah 50:4a).

An instructed tongue implies that it can be taught and learned. It's a skill we can attain. Let's **practice** giving words that bring life. We want to bring words of life that sustain the weary.

As we "treasure find" there is something in it for us as well! Have you ever seen this verse?

*My son, pay attention to what I say; listen closely to my words. Do not let them out of your sight, keep them within your heart; for they are life **to those who find them** and **health to a man's whole body*** (Proverbs 4:20–22).

The words *to those that find* according to Strong's 4672 means to those that "find what is lost; to discover; to light upon; to present; or to detect."

If you go on to study verse 22 it says, "health to a man's body." Yes, there is health to the man who comes into agreement with the truth, but also to you as you **find these things** and bring them to light (or help them be discovered again) It will bring healing to *your* body. The KJV says:

*"...unto **those that find them**...health to **all** their flesh."*

All means *all*. To all those who find them.

Wow! Anybody need healing? Anyone up for a treasure hunt?

So, we have some pretty great reasons to speak words of life. We have some pretty great reasons to treasure find—to **dig and decree**.

We do not want to be like psychics. We do not want to bewitch. We do not want to merely showboat our prophetic gift to look good and then leave people in our care in a worse "dust" state than before they came to us. Our job is to be a vessel of life to everyone in our path, and to be the prophetic voice God called us to be through love.

Galatians 5:6b states:

The only thing that counts is faith expressing itself through love.

Think on this

1. Which part of this chapter stands out to you **the** most?

2. Have you ever felt confused **after someone** ministered to you prophetically?

3. Ask the Lord to show you today how you can **be** used in your specific gifting in a "more excellent **way**" this week. List out these ways below.

4. What are some examples of words of life and words of purpose we can give to people during prophetic ministry?

5. Ask the Lord to show you areas where you may have mistakenly missed the mark and submit those to Him.

Prayerful Consideration

Lord thanks for your grace! Please allow us to speak words of Life. Instruct our tongue to speak the words you would want us to! Help us to walk in love as this is the more excellent way!

Amen

CHAPTER 5

How Can We Remove the Stumbling Blocks?

In the last chapter we discussed the ministry of "Angels that Gather" and how they are sent to remove stumbling blocks. Once the stumbling blocks are removed it leaves a clear path for people to walk forward in their destiny.

I believe we, too, can be used as instruments to remove these stumbling blocks and we will not have to depend on God to always send these particular angels.

First, we have a responsibility not to be the ones who put the blocks there in the first place! Right? But, if we come into contact with those who have these blocks how do we remove them?

Let's take a look at a couple of scriptures that many of you have probably studied for years and see if we can look at them with a new twist.

The weapons we fight with are not the weapons of the world. On the contrary, they have divine power to demolish strongholds (2 Corinthians 10:4).

This scripture indicates that our weapons are the opposite of the world's, by the phrase "On the contrary."

If our weapons, which are the opposite of the worlds, have the divine power to **demolish** strongholds, then the world's weapons must be the ones that helped to **put the strongholds up.**

We demolish arguments and every pretension that sets itself up against the knowledge of God, and we take captive every thought and make it obedient to Christ (2 Corinthians 10:5).

Here are some key words from this verse and their meanings:

Demolish: destruction of a stronghold or fortress

Stronghold: to hold fast to an argument in which you trust

Argument: calculation or reflection of one's conduct or rationalizations and excuses for strongholds

Pretension: something made up; a high and lofty fortress built **by an enemy**; **built proudly by an adversary**.

Set Itself: to lift our eyes, the focus of our worship

Look again at the scripture. It reads:

*We demolish arguments and **every** pretension that sets itself up against the knowledge of God and we take captive **every** thought and make it obedient to Christ.*

I have always read this scripture and applied it to my own life, pulling down *my own* strongholds and *my own* false ideas that have been set up.

These scriptures clearly state that we have the divine power of God to demolish strongholds. Not just our own. It says "**every** pretension" taking "**every** thought captive."

This scripture does not limit our weapons to our own strongholds.

Therefore, when we see a stronghold in someone else's life, for instance, we may see a false idea of who they think they are in Christ, or an ungodly idea that they have trusted in and believe, **we can demolish it!**

Whether near or far, in person or over a long distance, we can demolish it!

I can see a stumbling block in *someone else's way* and remove it out of *their* way!

How do we do this? We dig deep and decree.

Satan wants us to worship *him* and wants *his thoughts* to determine the direction of our lives…so what do we need to do? We stop allowing him to be the focus of our worship!

And what do we do with his thoughts? Demolish them! Destroy them! Stop entertaining them!

Dig deep, then decree what God says and believe what God says.

Come into agreement with the things He says about you and the plan for your life. Speak His plans over those you minister to. Help them come into agreement with them.

God Is Love

God is love, so we can substitute the word *love* for God in this sentence:

We demolish arguments and every pretension that sets itself up against the knowledge of Love.

Whose love? Our love. In other words, the knowledge or revelation of love from our Father in heaven.

We not only come against, we **demolish** the lies of the enemy that say "We cannot be loved by God," or "We are not lovable," or "God would not love us enough to give us great gifts or have a plan and future that is good for our lives."

Jesus tells His Father in John 17:26:

I have made you known to them, and will continue to make you known in order that the love you have for me may be in them and that I myself may be in them.

Jesus, who is the Spirit of Prophecy, is trying desperately to make God known to us. He so longs for us to know this revelation of love. He wants it firmly in us; the very same love that the Father has for Jesus, He has for us.

The weapons of the world fight against this revelation. Sometimes the weapons of the world are found in our own churches and pulpits.

Sometimes they come from our own mouths!

It's time to fight back!

To allow those thoughts is to consider them to be higher than the love of God and His plan and promises for us.

We use our divine and powerful weapons to help Jesus reveal this love.

For though we live in the world, we do not wage war as the world does (2 Corinthians 10:3).

Instead, *we live by* 2 Corinthians 10:5:

We demolish arguments and every pretension that sets itself up against the knowledge of God, and we take captive every thought and make it obedient to Christ.

The very next verse in the NKJV says this:

And having in a readiness to revenge all disobedience, when your obedience is fulfilled (2 Corinthians 10:6).

The phrase *in readiness* in Strong's 2092 means "to be prepared."

Revenge in Strong's 1556 means "to protect, to defend, to avenge a thing, to bring justice, to vindicate."

The word *disobedience* in Strong's 3976 means "hearing amiss."

The word *obedience* in Strong's 5218 means "an obedience showing the requirements of Christianity."

The phrase *is fulfilled* in Strong's 4137 means "to carry out, to execute a duty, to make complete and perfect to the end."

In other words, we need to be prepared with our divine and powerful weapons to bring justice and vindication to those who have heard false ideas about themselves.

We need to deliver truth to those who have heard amiss. This is one of our responsibilities as Christians. It is also one of the privileges of following Christ.

This is our commission.

So what does this mean?

First of all, we need to allow the spirit of prophecy in our churches instead of the worldly carnal weapons many of us have been using.

Revelation 19:10b states: *For the testimony of Jesus is the spirit of prophecy.*

What happens when we take out prophecy? We take out the very testimony of Jesus!

The spirit of prophecy is a major instrument for bringing justice and vindication to the false words many have heard both inside and outside church walls.

We also need to remember that we have the power to use these weapons for God's Kingdom to remind people who they are in Christ, not just in cases of our own strongholds, but for others and their strongholds.

Most importantly, this is our duty and responsibility as a Christian.

We will explore this more in the next chapter.

Think on this

1. Which part of this chapter stands out to you the most?

2. Read James 4:7… Write in your own words what this means to you.

So be subject to God. Resist the devil (stand firm against him) and he will flee from you (AMP).

3. How do you personally stand firm against the enemy and bring vindication for false strongholds in your own life?

4. How do you personally stand firm against the enemy and bring vindication for false strongholds in the lives of others?

5. Is there anything you need to change?

6. What kinds of weapons are demonstrated within your own church? In your home? At your work place? At your school? Are they energized by the spirit of prophecy or by the weapons of the world? Don't write anything down for this one, just think about it.

Prayerful Consideration

Lord we humbly ask for Your words of life to give to those You place in our lives.

Help us to hear from the spirit of prophecy in order for lives to be changed.

Help us to help You make Your love known to everyone we come in contact with.

Help us recognize that it is truly our privilege as Christians to vindicate and bring justice to the words that have been spoken falsely and to the words we have come into agreement with amiss.

This is our hearts' cry

In Jesus' name,

Amen

CHAPTER 6

An Agent of Change

In August 2004 the Lord gave me another vision similar to the "Dust" boy, except this time he showed me Proverbs 23:7a and He said these words, *"You are to be an Agent of Change."* He then took me back to the vision of the "Dust" boy highlighting the second prophetic person who had dug deep and decreed truth to him. This true prophetic voice had words on his forehead, and the words read, "Agent of Change."

The words "Agent of Change" rang in my mind and my heart.

Proverbs 23:7a (KJV) states:

*For as [a man] thinketh in his heart, **so is he**...*

If a man thinks he is dust he will manifest the dust or the *"so is he."* If a man thinks in his heart that he is stupid or cursed to live a life of anger he will manifest and demonstrate *"so is he."* If a man thinks he is a pig, he will sit in a pig-pen as the prodigal did.

Again, when the prodigal "came to himself" in Luke 15:17 it meant that he returned to himself. He remembered who he really was. If he had to return to himself, that indicates that who he had been portraying was not who he really was. The minute he "came to himself" within his heart, he manifested the true *"so is he"* by returning to his father and the beautiful life he had once left behind.

As we become Agents of Change we detect the treasures by digging below the surface. We then decree those things, changing the minds of those we minister to. By doing so, it leaves room for them to come into agreement with the treasures spoken and the "so is he" can manifest accordingly.

The word *agent*, according to Webster means: *an active force or substance producing an effect. A person empowered to act for another.*

We want to bring great positive effect. My absolute favorite verse in the bible is 1 Corinthians 15:10:

*But by the grace of God I am what I am, and His grace to me was **not without effect.***

I don't want to waste a single drop of the grace that has been given to me. I want to be as effective as I possibly can. We can all be effective by being Agents of Change.

Think on this

1. Which part of this chapter stands out to you the most?

2. Do you consider yourself an Agent of Change?

3. If not, ask yourself how you can be and list physical goals to accomplish this below.

4. Are there any specific negative ideas you have "thought in your own heart" that have manifested as "so is he"? List them below.

5. Now ask the Lord to give you the truths to defeat these lies and decree them over yourself.

6. Ask God to help you manifest the correct "so is he."

Prayerful Consideration

Lord, thank you for revealing your truth to us. Thanks for helping us be transformed by Your perfect grace in our lives. Please continue to reveal Yourself to us.

Amen

CHAPTER 7

False Prophets and Bad Fruit

Mathew 7:15–16 says:

"Watch out for false prophets. They come to you in sheep's clothing, but inwardly they are ferocious wolves. By their fruit you will recognize them.

Strong's 5578 describes the phrase "false prophet" in this section as one who utters falsehoods under the name of divine prophecy.

A falsehood is a lie, which is the opposite of the truth. The truth is the treasure. Our job is to speak the truth.

The scripture clearly says that it will come from people who really look like sheep or claim to be Christians. I don't know about you, but that makes me want to look into my own life and check myself!

Matthew 7:17–20 says:

Likewise every good tree bears good fruit, but a bad tree bears bad fruit. A good tree cannot bear bad fruit and a bad tree cannot bear good fruit. Every tree that does not bear good fruit is cut down and thrown into the fire. Thus, by their fruit you will recognize them.

What kind of fruit do we have? Are we getting people to come into agreement with lies? Or are we digging deep for the treasures of who God says they are?

Later in Matthew 7:21–23 it states:

*Not everyone who says to me, 'Lord, Lord,' will enter the kingdom of heaven, but only he who does the will of my Father who is in heaven. Many will say to me in that day, **'Lord, Lord, did we not prophesy in your name**, and in your name didn't we drive out demons and perform many miracles?' Then I will tell them plainly, 'I never knew you. Away from me, you evildoers!'*

Again, this sounds very serious. We must search out the truth and decree what God says.

Now, I am not expecting each of us to say every single word perfectly every time, especially if we are new to this prophetic life. God looks at the heart and motive.

Unfortunately, I think many people expect prophetic people to be born perfect and perform perfectly.

Interestingly enough we don't have the same expectations for firemen, policemen, teachers, preachers, or doctors. They all get time to learn their skill before they are sent out. Can you imagine if a doctor never got to practice before he cut you open?

There needs to be a safe place for prophetic voices to practice. A prophetic training school or a small group is a wonderful place to test out and learn not only how to hear, but how to speak out.

What we want to stay away from is just giving a diagnosis with no hope. Imagine the fright from having a doctor tell you, "You have cancer—*see ya*!" (Offering no hopeful prognosis.) I don't believe a lot of doctors would still be practicing medicine using this particular method.

We can do better than that through hard work and skillful training. We can truly have good fruit as we study our gift.

2 Timothy 2:15 (KJV) says:

Study to shew thyself approved...

One who was *approved* (in the Greek, "dokimos"), meant that they accepted no substitute for the real thing, no counterfeits. With study and training we can find the truth, decree the truth, and accept absolutely nothing but the truth. (So help us God!)

Think on this

1. Which part of this chapter stands out to you most?

2. What kind of fruit do you think you demonstrate?

3. What kind of fruit would your family or pastors say that you demonstrate?

4. What about your neighbors, friends, or co-workers? What kind of fruit would they say you demonstrate in your life?

5. What about strangers? Let's say at the post office? Grocery store? Local restaurant?

Prayerful Consideration

Lord, I humbly ask that you give us grace to bear good fruit. I want to be able to bear fruit that makes positive change. I want fruit that lasts. Please pour out Your grace.

Amen

CHAPTER 8

The Wrong Stuff?

How do we get caught up in prophesying the wrong stuff?

One reason we get caught in the trap of prophesying falsely is because we have been taught wrong as I mentioned in an earlier chapter discussing prophets versus psychics. I will say it again. Knowledge really is power.

Another reason this happens is due to the fact that we can sometimes prophesy out of our soul instead of our spirit. We can sometimes even do both!

An example of this happened when Jesus asked Peter the famous question in Matthew 16:15b:

"Who do you say I am?"

Peter's response was by the Spirit in verse 16:

"You are the Christ, the Son of the living God."
It was only a few moments later when Jesus told Peter and the disciples the truth of his coming suffering and death.

Peter's response in verse 22 was from his soul:

"Never Lord!" he said. "This shall never happen to you!"

Peter couldn't think of life without Jesus!

In verse 23 Jesus replies to Peter:

*"Get behind me Satan! You are **a stumbling block** to me; you do not have in mind the things of God, but the things of men."*

Notice one moment Peter was speaking words of God and the next he was a "stumbling block."

See how easy it can be to go in and out of being Spirit-led?

If Peter can do it, how easy would it be for us to do it?

Also, notice the words Jesus used *"You are **a stumbling block** to me."*

This is the same phrase used in Luke 17:1–3a discussed earlier:

Then He said unto the disciples, It is impossible but that offenses will come: but woe unto him, through *whom they come! It were better for him that a millstone were hanged about his neck, and he cast into the sea, than that he should **offend** one of these little ones! Take heed to yourselves... (KJV).*

Again, the word *offend* here in Strong's 4625 means to put a **stumbling block** or impediment in the way of another who may trip and fall, or to cause a person to begin to distrust one whom he ought to trust and obey.

We must be careful to remain in the Spirit of the Lord, to have the mind of the Lord, and to be Spirit-led **moment to moment**.

Think on this

1. Which part of this chapter stands out to you the most?

2. Ask the Lord to bring to your remembrance if there was ever a time that you prophesied out of your soul.

3. What are some ways we can "watch ourselves" (or take heed)?

4. What are some ways we can remain in the Spirit moment to moment?

Prayerful Consideration

Lord, I pray that from this moment on I would be aware of everything that goes into my mind and everything that comes out of my mouth. Lord I pray you would help my to discern and filter any wrong teaching from my heart. Help me discern truth from false teachings in order for me to move forward in great power for your kingdom!

Amen

CHAPTER 9

Second Heaven Information vs. Third Heaven Revelation

Another reason why we sometimes fail to see the treasures inside people is because we see and hear from the second heaven instead of getting third heaven revelation.

A few months ago, I heard about a man who told a woman that every time he prayed for her, he saw a skull and crossbones over her head in the spirit. *Hmmmm.* Very encouraging wouldn't you say?

This "prophetic voice" offered no hope or interpretation of the impression received. "Nope, just skull and crossbones…that's it."

Well, what kind of dusty, cloudy state do you think this

woman was in after hearing this information? She called me in a panicked state!

This kind of word opens a door in the spirit realm to fear. (Remember the target on the chest of "Dust" boy?) Once the door is open, the victimized person becomes an open target for demonic attack in every way.

I believe the skull and crossbones picture was second heaven information that the guy picked up in the spirit. He was describing a plot to come against her. If the guy could have pressed through he may have gone higher for the third heaven revelation that this woman was actually a giver of life.

So what do you do if you only receive second heaven information? Well, my first thought is to try hard to press through for third heaven revelation. With proper training you really can accomplish this in many cases.

Why would God allow you to see and hear second heaven information? If this type of information is all you usually get then realize that the Lord must have allowed you to intercept it because He has also given you the keys and authority to stop and break the plans of the enemy.

For instance, if you work in an office as a manager on duty and you see a tissue box in the wrong place, you have the authority to put it back in its place. Don't you? This same authority applies to anything—book keeping, cleaning, furniture placement, equipment replacement, etc. It also applies to the spirit world.

If you see it, then you can fix it because you are in a

position of authority to do so. As long as it is in your territory and as long as it is in your face, you have authority.

I believe it is the same in the spirit, that God would not have allowed you to see the problem if He wasn't also giving you a solution: **you**.

Here is another example:

One time when I was ministering to a woman in a corporate worship setting, the Lord revealed to me that she was not reading her bible. Why did He show me that? So that I would openly expose her and embarrass her in front of the entire congregation?

No! God doesn't allow us to see things for "show and tell." He doesn't allow us to see things just for the fun of it either. There is purpose in everything he does!

He was showing me that His heart was for her to spend more time in His precious Word so that she would transform her mind and become closer to Him. His desire was for her to grow and mature in Him and the way for her to do that was through reading His Word. His desire for her was that she would know Him more, and spend more time with Him. He missed her and longed for her.

Now, did I even need to say that? Would that bring her public condemnation or life?

Because He showed me that, He also gave me the keys to cause her spirit to birth a new desire and passion for the Word.

This is what I said:

"I see you in the middle of a beautiful vivid field of green grass, which represents the word of God, and I feel like the Lord is saying that He is imparting to you, right now, a newness and freshness in the midst of His Word. I know you are a woman of the Word, but you are coming to a new season where everything in His Word will come alive in new ways for you. You will find yourself in the depths of His Word like never before and with that comes the understanding, clearer than you even have now, today."

As I called this forth into the atmosphere, I actually felt the impartation. I saw it hit her and change her on the inside.

Now, notice I didn't once say that she wasn't reading her bible. Notice too, that I kept on emphasizing the fact that it would be even more than what she was already doing. (This was a true statement as she was doing nothing—but you don't have to say that, do you?)

I could have exposed her, but I know inside her heart she was thinking, "What? I have not read my bible in six months. Why didn't she expose me?" And in the process, she felt the tender grace of the Lord pursuing her for more time than she had been giving Him.

See, the Lord said she was a "woman of the Word." He called forth those true things that are found deeper than the surface dust. He knew she was deep down a woman of the Word and part of her calling needed that called out and birthed in order for her to move on.

Shame could not have done that. Condemnation could not have done that. Those things are not the voice of the Father, but the voice of the accuser saying "It is never enough." "You are never enough."

Romans 2:4b states:

…God's kindness leads you toward repentance.

First Timothy 5:1–2 says:

*Do not rebuke an **older man** harshly, but exhort him as if he were your father. Treat **younger men** as brothers, **older women** as mothers, and **younger women** as sisters, with absolute purity.*

I think that pretty much covers everyone.

Other reasons why God will allow you to intercept second heaven information are to train you up and sometimes just to give you an opportunity to have an intimate moment with your Father in heaven.

See, God can do anything He wants, but there are times when He wants to do something *with* you. Sometimes He wants you to partake with Him in the opportunity to bring change and help others who need Him.

For example, my four-year-old loves to help sweep the floor. If she sees me get out the broom, in a split-second she has her miniature-sized toy broom out to use right alongside mine.

This usually takes me twice as long and sometimes even creates a bit more of a mess, but watching the excitement of her being able to help is priceless.

Imagine how much more our heavenly Father delights in watching us help Him sweep out the "dust" in the lives of others. He wants to bond with us. He wants us to take part.

In doing so, the feeling of being able to bring eternal change in someone's life is amazing. There are no words to describe it. Those are the moments when you honestly look to the heavens and humbly say, "Lord, how could You have just let me help You do that?" And then you can hardly wait for the next opportunity to come!

Haven't we all been there?

So, reach for third heaven when possible but if it isn't there, don't wonder why, just use what you have and work with God to make an impact! You can do it! We will discuss how in more detail in the next chapter.

Think on this

1. Which part of this chapter stands out to you the most?

2. Have you ever received second heaven information?

3. Look up the word *kind* in the dictionary and record the definition.

4. Do you consider yourself to be a kind person?

5. Why? What do you do to show kindness to others?

6. Would others say they consider you a kind person? (Especially those in your life who do not know Jesus personally.)

7. What are some new ways you can demonstrate kindness to someone this week through your words or actions?

8. Think of a time from your childhood when you and your parents accomplished a task together. Write down the memory of it.

9. Think of an intimate time when your heavenly Father let you help Him help someone else in need. How did it make you feel?

Prayerful Consideration

Lord, I pray today that You would help us to be kind to others. Help us to look for ways to be Your hands extended to every person You place in our realm of care moment to moment. You are a blessing to me Lord. Help me be a blessing to others.

Amen

CHAPTER 10

Only Second Heaven Information?

What do you do if you have really tried and can only see second heaven information?

If you have only received second heaven information:

1. Press In

Jeremiah 33:3 encourages us:

'Call to Me, and I will answer you, and show you great and mighty things, which you do not know' (NKJV).

The Amplified bible says it like this:

Call to Me and I will answer you and show you great and mighty things, fenced in and hidden, which you do not know (do not distinguish and recognize, have knowledge of and understand).

He so longs to show us things we do not know, great and mighty things that are fenced in and not recognized. The **condition** and **requirement** is the *asking.*

Take time to cry out to Him. I mean **really** cry out to Him. When is the last time you have done that?

I believe God can and will honor your heart's cry.

2. Assume the Opposite

If you have tried to cry out and still cannot go higher than second heaven, then assume that God's heart and plan is the opposite of what you hear. If you see darkness, then you know it is the enemy's plan.

If you know the enemy's plan, then you can assume that God's plan would be the opposite. Ask the Lord how to speak out the opposite of the enemy's plan in order to birth the new to the surface and then pray for the person to see that manifestation. (Or the "so is he.") Your voice and words are weapons. They are life and death.

Proverbs 18:21 says:

Death and life are in the power of the tongue: and they that love it shall eat the fruit thereof (KJV).

Genesis 1:3 says:

And God said, "Let there be light," and there was light.

Genesis 1:26 says:

And God said, "Let us make man in our image, after our likeness..." (KJV).

Genesis 1:27 says:

So God created man in his own image, in the image of God created he him; male and female created he them (KJV).

If we are created in His image, we can do the very same things he has done by speaking light and life into a situation.

If you see darkness, speak the opposite of what you see in order for it to be established.

For example, one time when we were out on the streets doing prophetic evangelism, we ran into a character that was so full of manipulation that his soul almost leaked it. He really wanted to get a "spiritual reading" from our table but all I could see was this manipulation.

I waited on the Lord as long as I could, but sometimes you don't have much time, especially in street ministry. If a life of manipulation was Satan's plan, what could be God's plan for this young man?

I realized by the grace of God that he actually had a gift of influence and that he was a very strong leader. If this leadership gift was submitted to God it could be a powerful tool for heaven. Instead, it was being used by the enemy.

So you minister the plan of God. You minister the

opposite of the information you have intercepted from the second heaven revelation.

You say that this young man is a strong leader and is born to influence others to positive things. You may also caution him by saying that great leadership gifts also bring great responsibility and see where it goes. In my experience, speaking life, love, and truth first opens a door for conversation. You have to press in for Daddy's perfect words and timing. He knows exactly what to say!

3. Submit your Gift

Sometimes when there seems to be a "clog" in revelation from Him, I recommend consciously giving your prophetic gift back to the Lord. Let me explain:

When my little girl was even smaller than she is now, she used to carry around this little pink eraser everywhere she went. It was something I picked up at the store one day and gave to her because I could tell she really admired it. She ate with it, slept with it, and wore the thing out carrying it around. After a while it started to look like it needed a makeover!

One day, while Shaen was playing with her eraser, she suddenly came over and handed it to me. With tears in her eyes she said, "Momma, I want you to have this."

I could tell she didn't want to give it up. It was her most prized possession! I told her lovingly just to keep it and handed it back, giving her a hug.

Shaen then looked at me very seriously and said,

"No, Momma, you are supposed to have it."

I didn't know what to say. I certainly didn't have any use for it and didn't even want it! What was I going to do with this ratty pink eraser? But you could tell it was important for her to give it to me. So, finally I did take it from her and thanked her with tears in *my* eyes for her sacrifice by giving so generously. She touched something in me that warmed my heart.

The next day, I told her that I felt that since she was a big girl in giving away her favorite toy that I thought she needed to have it back. This time with joy she excitedly received it back.

I thought about the process and saw the comparison to the way God is. It reminded me of when I was a little girl at Christmas time. My sister and I were always so excited to get gifts, but more exciting for me was giving them!

Looking back now as an adult it was a crazy set up, but my Mom and Dad would give **us** money to buy **their** gifts, so we felt like we were a part of the process of giving. Being four or five years old, I felt so mature to be able to do that for my parents—and it was their money all along!

This is how God is. He is so generous! My husband, Stephen, says we are like renters! We get to use all God's stuff while we are here! He not only gives us things but I believe He enjoys the process as much as we do.

Going back to my third suggestion, if you feel as

though you are not able to receive from Him like you wish you could, maybe it is because you have not fully submitted your gift back to Him.

4. Seek the Father's Heart

Another reason why we may not be getting the revelation we could be is because we lack an understanding of the Father's heart. This is a must for ministry. It is not always an overnight revelation either, especially if you didn't have it modeled correctly from your own parents. There are several great teachings and books out there that can help, but if you want it from the Lord Himself, ask Him for it! He will honor your prayer! This is a crucial part of effective ministry. I cannot stress this enough!

5. Pursue More Training

The last thing I will suggest is more training. We can always use more training. We will discuss this in the next chapter.

Think on this

1. Which part of this chapter stands out to you the most?

2. Have you ever submitted your gift or gifts to Him?

3. Do you feel as though you have a full understanding of the Father's heart for you and for others?

Prayerful Consideration

*Lord, please help me to press in for Your perfect revelation. I want more than second heaven information; I want Your heart for people. Lord, I pray that even as I minister people would feel Your love and presence causing everyone around me to want to know You more. Lord, please help me submit my gift to You. Help me submit my **life** to You!*

Amen

CHAPTER 11

Any Two-Year-Old Can See and Say

Remember what the Lord told me?

He said, *"Any two-year-old can See and Say."*

First Corinthians 3:1–3 says:

Brothers, I could not address you as spiritual but as worldly—mere infants in Christ.

I gave you milk, not solid food, for you were not yet ready for it.

Indeed, you are still not ready. You are still worldly.

According to Strong's 4561 the word *worldly* means "seated in the animal nature, governed by human nature, not by the Spirit of God."

Paul says in 1 Corinthians 13:11:

When I was a child, I talked like a child, I thought like a child, I reasoned like a child. When I became a man, I put childish ways behind me.

In this verse, the word *child*, according to Strong's 2031 means "infant, little, untaught, unskilled."

We can be trained. We can be taught to move forward in our gifting in Christ. All it takes is a little practice.

Hebrews 5:11–14 says:

We have much to say about this, but it is hard to explain because you are slow to learn. In fact, though by this time you ought to be teachers, you need someone to teach you the elementary truths of God's word all over again.

You need milk, not solid food! Anyone who lives on milk, being still an infant, is not acquainted with the teaching about righteousness.

*But solid food is for the mature, who by **constant use** have **trained themselves** to distinguish good from evil.*

Righteousness means "the right things of God" according to Strong's 1342. We definitely want to be acquainted with the teachings about the "right things of God." Don't we?

Also, notice it says we are mature because of **constant use** and through **training ourselves**. We have a responsibility here.

What is our responsibility? Exercising our gifts and studying.

Think on this

1. Which part of this chapter stands out to you the most?

2. Do you consider yourself to be on spiritual milk or solid food? Explain your answer.

3. What are the gifts God has given you?

4. Have you taken time to study them?

Prayerful Consideration

Lord, thank you for this revelation. I pray You would show us the areas of our gifting in order for us to study and train responsibly. We want to be good stewards of what You have given us. Help us to do this.

Amen

CHAPTER 12

All By Myself

One more thing I would like to address before we close. There are going to be times in your life when you feel a little on the "dusty" side and you will not necessarily have a prophetic person around to help get you out of the dust.

If you have studied the life of David, you will see that he went through his own challenges in this area. Have you read the Psalms lately?

When these times come, the same techniques we have talked about in previous chapters apply, except we have to use these techniques to minister to **ourselves**.

First Samuel 30:6b (KJV) says:

David encouraged himself in the LORD his God.

When you feel the dust of the earth starting to cling, we cannot come into agreement with worldly strongholds. We must pursue God's plan and heart for us and decree them over **ourselves**.

If you really think about it, we are bombarded with negativity from the moment our feet hit the ground every single day: from the news, television, billboards, magazines, not to mention people!

A big help to keep us "clean" is to keep our hearts focused on God and His heart and plan for us. When the arrows try to come we have to hold fast to what God says about us and speak that out! Decree His words over our hearts and our lives and dispel the opposite.

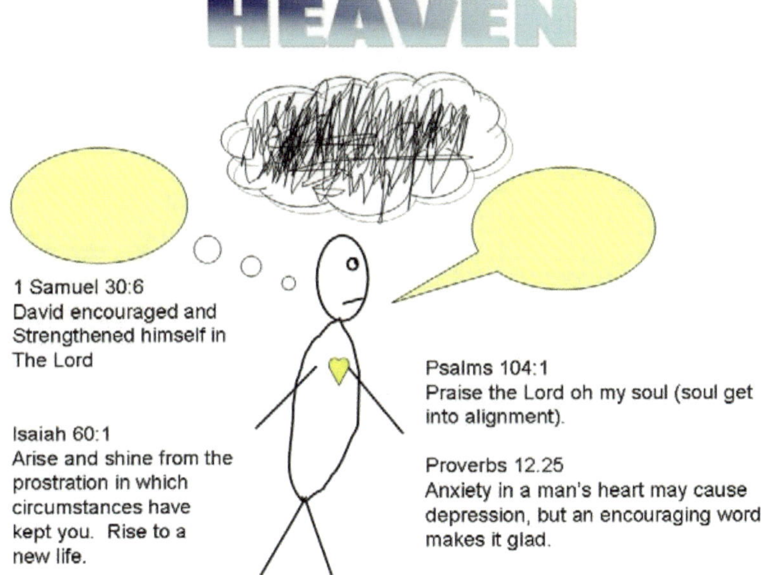

Illustration #10

Illustration #11

Think on this

1. Which part of this chapter stands out to you the most?

2. Have you ever felt the weight of negativity trying to "dust" you over? If so, how did you handle it?

3. What will you do now?

4. Have you ever asked God what His plan is for you? Have you asked Him how He sees you? Take a few minutes now. Ask Him to reveal His heart for you, His love for you, and His plan for you. Write down what He says! It is powerful!

Prayerful Consideration

Lord, help us to be aware of the attacks of the enemy to get us to agree with his lies. I pray You will give us the grace to keep our mind, focus and peace on You and Your plan for us. Lord, please show us how You see us! We want to know Your plan. We want desperately to understand Your unconditional love for us. Please begin the process now.

Amen

Conclusion

You see, we are not to *See and Say* as it may lead to *Speaking and Spelling*. Sometimes we are only to *See and Pray*. Mostly we are to *Dig and Decree*! The higher prophetic calling is to be a treasure finder.

If you have had your eyes opened to the revelation of God and His way to prophesy…

If you want to move forward in the things of God by the Spirit and not the soul moment to moment…

If you want to use wisdom in the words you choose to speak over someone in order to glorify God…

If you honestly desire the mature things of God and want to put away childish things…

Join me in this prayer:

Lord, forgive me if I have used the prophetic in a way that did not please You. I did not know what I was doing. The longing of my heart is to move, to act, and to will according to Your perfect ways. I only want to do as You say, go where You go, and say what You say

Help me Lord to be a vessel for Your Kingdom. Help me to bring life and fruit to anyone and everyone You place in my care here on earth.

Give me words of life to help transform people's lives. Give me specific details that will pierce their hearts and launch them into their destiny in great power.

*You are a mighty powerful God who deserves all glory and honor. Please Lord, help me represent You the way You would want to be represented moment to moment. Let me be guided by Your Spirit of Truth **moment to moment**.*

Amen

Homework

Now that you have come to understand another level of the prophetic gift and how to use it, you must put it into practice.

Philippians 4:9 says:

Whatever you have learned or received or heard from me, or seen in me—put it into practice. And the God of peace will be with you.

Matthew 7:24 says:

Therefore everyone who hears these words of mine and puts them into practice is like a wise man who built his house on the rock.

Some of the ways I have encouraged groups or individuals to practice are included in the following three assignments:

Assignment A

Call a group of friends. Arrange a get-together and ask them to be prepared to bring a magazine picture of something negative, e.g., an alcohol or cigarette advertisement, showing something "sinful."

When you and your friends get together, get out the pictures each of you brought and pretend these pictures are the impressions you have received from the Holy Spirit for someone you are practicing ministering to. How would you minister to the person? What words would you say in order to bring life and not exposure? Dig deep for the mature encouraging words that unlock the people from the chains of the enemy. Remember: "If you see it and it's in your face, God is using you to put it into place." Use your authority!

Assignment B

Practice quietly at the mall or grocery store. Put up your spiritual antennae and if you see negative things, turn them inside out. Practice in your mind how you would speak to these people in order for God to touch them and bring permanent transformation in their lives. Be creative! If you do not see yourself as creative, turn to the **Creator** who is in you. He will surely give you words of life to speak.

Assignment C

As you have met the challenge of digging and decreeing life into darkness, hit the streets with a group. Use your tools to bring change in your own community. I would recommend separating into groups of no more than three so you would not overwhelm a stranger. Have others stand farther away, interceding for you and your group. Then watch God go!

(If you are interested in hosting a prophetic evangelism workshop to get more training in this area, you can go to www.swiftfire.org or email info@swiftfire.org for more information.)

Testimonies

If you have any testimonies as a result of reading this book, please let us know! We would love to hear from you!

Send your testimonies to info@swiftfire.org. Or write to:

Swiftfire Ministries International
1113 S. Range Ave
Ste 110 Box 333
Denham Springs, La. 70726
www.swiftfire.org

We are very interested in what God is doing through your lives as a result of this book.

We are the Bionic Bride! We are the ones called
to do GREATER THINGS than Jesus did!
We are all born supernatural beings! We just need
to believe and understand what that looks like for us!

Join Sharnael in this teaching providing insight on how
we, too, can step into the call of God on our lives in the
arena of the supernatural.

For more information on this product and more,
visit swiftfire.org

God is Speaking... Do You Understand His Language?

Join Sharnael in this revolutionary teaching uncovering key truths within the supernatural. You, too, can shift the world with these innovative revelations!

If you want to see, hear, understand and move in power like never before this book is for you!

For more information on this product and more, visit swiftfire.org

swiftfire ministries
international
overcoming the
Religious Spirit
2 CD Set

swiftfire ministries
international
swiftfire.org
225.791.7696
Sharnael Wolverton
"Moving from Shaking
to Groundbreaking"

Some of us are called to be trail blazers, pioneers, trend setters, REVOLUTIONISTS! Sharnael's teaching "Spirit of a Revolutionist" gives inside understanding to this precious call! Dive in and see the power of God revolutionize your life!

For more information on this product and more, visit swiftfire.org

"What is Breakthrough" provides hope and courage
to those in a place of desperately needing change
for their situation! Listen and receive necessary
words of life to revive your soul!

For more information on this product and more,
visit swiftfire.org

Plan Now to Attend Our Next Louisiana AmpliFIRE Conference!

Sharnael Wolverton and the Swiftfire Ministries International team welcome you to come and receive ministry from the Holy Spirit at one of our meetings here in Louisiana.

It is a great time of awesome worship, prophetic kingdom messages and personal ministry time! It is a wonderful time to meet with Him as well as meet new friends.

Make time to get away from your busy schedule and be rejuvenated in His presence!

For more information about our next meeting visit our website at:

www.swiftfire.org

Swiftfire Ministries International Information:

God's vision for Swiftfire Ministries International is that we would effectively help people recognize who they are in Christ and to guide them into the fullness of who they are. This is done in order for each one to carry out the purposes of God moment to moment.

Swiftfire's mission is to do this through: itinerant ministry, conferences, schools, workshops, mission trips, outreaches, prophetic evangelism, dream interpretation, counseling, intercession, bible study, discipleship, media, music, dance, art, and both personal and team ministry.

Sharnael also feels God is calling us to a place of more unity within the body. She desires to network and connect leaders, pastors, itinerants, churches, mission groups, and "marketplace missionaries" not only state-wide but internationally. **Kingdom unity and relationship is key for effective change.**

For More Information:

Swiftfire Ministries International
1113 S Range Ave
STE 110 Box 333
Denham Springs La. 70726

www.swiftfire.org

Booking Information

If you would like to book Sharnael Wolverton for your next conference, church meeting or retreat, please contact her at the address below. If you would like to become a "Fire Starter" (A Swiftfire Ministries International Partner) please contact us at:

Swiftfire Ministries International
1113 S Range Ave
STE 110 Box 333
Denham Springs La. 70726

www.swiftfire.org
info@swiftfire.org

About the Author

Sharnael Wolverton of Swiftfire Ministries International was called to the ministry at an early age. In her pursuit for God, she went into a place of "the school of the Holy Spirit." During this period of seeking intimacy with Him, she encountered many dreams, visions, visitations, and divine appointments leading to the birthing of Swiftfire Ministries International. As she continues to lean into Him, she ministers and teaches under the prophetic anointing, causing revelation, activation, miracles, signs and wonders, and healing.

Sharnael not only has a heart for Kingdom ministry and training though speaking at conferences, teaching workshops, writing and hosting her television show "Swiftfire with Sharnael Wolverton" she also has a focus and heart for the war on poverty. Her passion for orphans, widows, and single mothers has been a driving force for her raising finances to help in the area of these people groups.

Locally, since she is strategically located North of New Orleans, Louisiana, where there have been awesome opportunities for ministry to those post Katrina and Rita victims. Many have relocated and started over in the area she currently resides. These people are very much still in need.

Internationally, she has been involved in several mission team groups over the last two decades and continues to raise support with a goal of building ten orphanages (Partnering with Wes and Stacey Campbell).

Sharnael is very excited about the potential of the New Church and fresh ways the church can reach out. She offers both financial and governmental leadership support to "out of the box" coffee shop churches, home groups, media churches, new church plants and training centers but equally supports the radiant "traditional" churches. Both variety and creativity are crucial to reach the world.

If you are interested in becoming a financial partner or prayer partner for any of these areas of her ministry please go to the website at www.swiftfire.org to learn more. Or write to info@swiftfire.org.